50⁺ Super-Fun Math Activities

SCHOLA

GRADE 4

by Jack Silbert

NEW YORK • TORONTO • LONDON • AUCKLAND • SYDNEY
MEXICO CITY • NEW DELHI • HONG KONG • BUENOS AIRES

Teaching *Resources*

Edited by Jean Liccione

Cover design by Ka-Yeon Kim-Li

Interior design by Ellen Matlach Hassell for Boultinghouse & Boultinghouse, Inc.

Interior illustrations by Maxie Chambliss and Manuel Rivera

ISBN-13: 978-0-545-20819-2

ISBN-10: 0-545-20819-X

2 3 4 5 6 7 8 9 10   40   17 16 15 14 13 12 11 10

Contents

(continued on the next page)

✳ This activity includes a reproducible.

✳ This activity includes a reproducible.

Introduction

Welcome to *50+ Super-Fun Math Activities: Grade 4*. This book contains a unique collection of activities that reinforce important first-grade-level mathematics concepts and skills and support the math standards recommended by the National Council of Teachers of Mathematics (NCTM). See page 6, for more.

The book is organized by nine major content topics. When you're teaching a particular math concept or skill, just check the Contents page. Browse the activities listed under each topic to find just the right one to reinforce students' learning. Each major topic has projects, games, activities, and ready-to-use reproducibles designed to reinforce specific learning objectives. The activities will also get students interested and excited, and encourage them to value math and become confident mathematicians.

ACTIVITY FEATURES

The activities include grouping suggestions, lists of needed materials, teaching tips, step-by-step directions, and easy Assessment ideas. Some activities also include the following features:

◆ Extensions and Variations—ideas for taking the math skills and concepts further

◆ Home Links—quick and easy activities students can do at home with their families

◆ Writing Connections—suggestions for encouraging students to communicate and reinforce what they've learned through writing.

ABOUT GROUPING

Sometimes it's important for students to work together in groups or pairs, to collaborate and communicate. Sometimes they need to work independently. The activities in this book support a variety of needs, from independent to whole class work. You'll find a grouping suggestion at the beginning of each activity.

ASSESSING STUDENTS' WORK

NCTM recommends a variety of approaches to assessment of the various dimensions of a student's mathematical learning. The following assessment suggestions are incorporated throughout this book:

◆ ideas for group and class discussion

◆ ideas for journal writing and written response

◆ ideas for ongoing informal teacher observations

On pages 61–63, you'll also find suggested ways of observing and keeping records of students' work as well as a reproducible student Self-Evaluation Form and an Assessment Checklist and Scoring Rubric.

Remember that you can review students' self-assessments and their journals and written responses to see not only how well they understand concepts but also how well they express their mathematical understandings.

CONNECTIONS TO THE MATH STANDARDS

The activities in this book are designed to support you in meeting the following process standards for students in grades 3–5 recommended by the National Council of Teachers of Mathematics (NCTM):

Problem Solving The activities promote a problem-solving approach to learning. Throughout the book, you'll find suggestions for encouraging students to develop, apply, and explain their problem-solving strategies.

Reasoning & Proof Suggestions in the last step of each activity can serve as prompts to help students draw logical conclusions, explain and justify their thinking, and "pull it together" to make sense of the mathematics skills and concepts they've just used. Activities encourage students to use patterns and relationships as they work.

Communication Activities include ideas for helping students organize and consolidate their mathematical thinking through class discussions and writing connections.

Connections Activities tie to the real world, to the interests of fourth-grade students, and to other areas of the curriculum. The purpose of many activities is to bridge conceptual and procedural knowledge, and to bridge different topics in mathematics.

Representation Students use manipulatives, pictures and diagrams, and numerical representations to complete the activities.

The grids below show how the activities correlate to the other Standards for Grades 3–5.

PAGE	Number & Operations	Algebra	Geometry	Measurement	Data Analysis & Probability
8	◆				
9	◆				
10	◆				
12	◆				
13	◆				
14	◆				
15	◆				
17				◆	
18	◆			◆	
19	◆				
21					
23	◆				
24	◆				
26	◆				
27	◆				
29	◆				◆

PAGE	Number & Operations	Algebra	Geometry	Measurement	Data Analysis & Probability
31	◆				◆
32	◆	◆	◆	◆	
33	◆	◆	◆	◆	
34			◆		
35	◆	◆	◆		
37			◆		◆
39			◆	◆	
41				◆	
43				◆	
45	◆	◆			
46	◆	◆			
47	◆				
49					
50					
52	◆			◆	
53				◆	

PAGE	Number & Operations	Algebra	Geometry	Measurement	Data Analysis & Probability
54	◆			◆	
56					◆
58					◆
59		◆			◆
60	◆	◆	◆	◆	

Source: National Council of Teachers of Mathematics. (2000). *Principles and standards for school mathematics*. Reston: VA: NCTM. www.nctm.org

Any Time Is Math Time

Use these quick activities when you have just a few minutes to fill!

1. IT'S A PLEASURE TO MEASURE!

Instead of calling out "here!" when you take attendance, have students call out a unit of measurement. If they get stuck, prompt them with types of measurement: How do we measure time? weight? distance?

2. WEATHER PATTERNS

If your class reports on the weather as part of their daily routine, use the day's expected high temperature and challenge the class to raise it with a round-robin addition activity. Have the first student add a specified number to the temperature. The next student adds the same number to the new temperature, and so on. (Early in the year, try simple patterns, such as adding 2. Work up to larger numbers.) If the day's temperature is high, reverse the process by subtracting from the high temperature.

3. MATHY BIRTHDAY TO YOU!

Have students call out their birth month and day in numbers. (Example: 3/27 for March 27.) Ask them to perform a calculation with those digits, using the skill you are concentrating on at the time. For example, ask students to multiply with 3, 2, and 7 (3 x 2 x 7 = 42). As the year progresses, ask students to use more than one operation.

4. GET BETTER WITH LETTERS

As students count off, ask them to also say a noun that begins with the same letter as their numbers. (Examples: one ostrich, two tigers, three trees, four frogs.)

5. ANGLING FOR EXERCISE

Have students stand up and spread out a bit. Call out angle classifications (right, acute, obtuse) and have students form these types of angles with their arms. As students grow more comfortable with angles, call out degree measures and have students approximate those angles.

6. TIME FLIES!

Have one student say the current time. Successive students should add a specified number of minutes to the time (10:51, 10:58, 11:05, 11:12, etc.).

7. MONEY IN MOTION

Give students a starting amount of money, such as $3. Have students in turn add successive denominations (penny, nickel, dime, quarter; penny, nickel, dime, quarter) until reaching a specified amount. The remaining students now reverse the order until a penny is reached, and so on.

8. FRACTION ACTION PARTNERS

When students are pairing off for an activity, have one student call out any fraction. The partner should call out the reciprocal of that fraction (3/5 – 5/3, etc.).

Once Upon a Number...

In this story-writing activity, students will find numbers from when they rise to when they slumber.

Grouping

Individual

You'll Need

◆ Paper
◆ Pencils

Teaching Tip

This activity can be done in class or as a homework assignment.

DIRECTIONS

1. Ask students to think about all the numbers in their lives—age, weight, date of birth, height, street address, phone number, etc. Invite students to write a brief "number autobiography." They should tell all about themselves, using as many number facts as they can. You may want to do this as a timed writing exercise, or place a limit on the number of pages or words. You could also specify a minimum number of numbers.

2. When their autobiographies are complete, ask for volunteers to read their stories aloud to the class. (If any students are uncomfortable sharing certain number facts, allow them to "edit" certain sentences for a read-aloud.)

3. While one student is reading, ask the others to listen closely and jot down the various uses of numbers. Afterward, call on students to tell the different uses they heard and make a list on the chalkboard.

4. Discuss the importance of labels with numbers: they give numbers meaning. (The boy is 5 feet tall versus The boy is 5 tall.) Have students look for the labels next to the numbers in their own stories, or add them if necessary.

ASSESSMENT

For a self-assessment, have students circle all the numbers and labels in their stories. Are the numbers accurate? Do all the numbers have labels?

▶▶▶ EXTENSION

Have students interview a friend or family member and write a number story about that person's life.

In the Right Place

**Students will "stand up and be counted"
as they cover the basics of place value!**

PREPARATION

On large separate pieces of paper, use magic markers to write the digits 0 to 9, and the words *ones, tens, hundreds, thousands,* etc. (depending on which place value you want to teach to). Also draw commas on 1 or 2 sheets.

DIRECTIONS

1. On the chalkboard, write a number as large as the place value you want to teach. Write the name of the place value under each digit. Point to each place and review what it represents. Then ask questions such as: Which number is in the thousands place? What does the first 3 represent?

3	4	8,	7	2	3
hundred thousands place	ten thousands place	thousands place	hundreds place	tens place	ones place

2. Select students to represent the various places that you have designated. Give the papers with the matching word to the "place-value" students. Also select "comma" students. Have the students pin the papers to their shirts. Then have the "place-value" and "comma" students come to the front of the class, and ask the other students to direct them to their proper positions.

3. Pass out the sheets with the digits to other students. Say a number and ask the class to direct the digits to their correct places.

4. Repeat the activity with a variety of smaller and larger numbers. Each time, invite a different group of students to carry numbers. When students have grown confident in the activity, try it without the place-value word signs.

ASSESSMENT

If individual students are not participating, ask them specific questions, such as, Which number is in the thousands place?

⇥⇥⇥ EXTENSION

Use the same activity to reinforce decimal place value—tenths, hundredths, thousandths, etc. This time, include a student to represent the decimal point.

Grouping

Whole class

You'll Need

◆ Paper
◆ Markers
◆ Safety pins or paper clips

Teaching Tip

Be sure to include zero in a variety of places.

Space-Chase Place Value

Students use strategies to capture creepy space creatures while learning about place value.

DIRECTIONS

1. Review place value to the hundred thousands place with students. Tell them they will need this knowledge if they want to do well in the Space Chase game.

2. Distribute reproducible page 11 to each pair. Demonstrate how to use the spinner by spinning a paper clip around a pencil placed at the spinner's center. Players should spin to see who goes first, with the higher spin going first. Players then take turns spinning.

3. On each turn, a player spins and lands on a number. The player then says which creepy space creature he or she will capture on that turn. Players write the number they landed on in the blank that corresponds with the place value of the space creature. (For example: In round 1, Player 1 spins a 5. She decides to capture a Kerpew on this turn. Kerpews represent the ten thousands place. So Player 1 writes a 5 in the ten thousands place of her Round 1 score blanks.) Players record their numbers in the score blanks of the round they are playing.

4. A particular space creature can be captured only once per round. The round ends when both players have captured all six space creatures. Play continues for three rounds. The winner of each round is the player who has written the greater 6-digit number.

ASSESSMENT

Observe which students are developing a strategy to succeed at this game. If a student lands on a high number, he or she should probably place it in the hundred thousands place. A player placing a 1 in the hundred thousands place may not be clear on the game's concept.

Hundred Thousands	Ten Thousands	Thousands	Hundreds	Tens	Ones
1	2	3,	4	5	6

Space-Chase Place Value

FLOOZOP
Hundred Thousands Place

REMEMBER!

KERPEW
Ten Thousands Place

MEEKEEWEE
Thousands Place

GLUND
Hundreds Place

SCANTZNOB
Tens Place

VIG
Ones Place

SCORE	**SCORE**
Player 1: _____ (Name)	Player 2: _____ (Name)
Round 1: ___ ___ ___, ___ ___ ___	Round 1: ___ ___ ___, ___ ___ ___
Round 2: ___ ___ ___, ___ ___ ___	Round 2: ___ ___ ___, ___ ___ ___
Round 3: ___ ___ ___, ___ ___ ___	Round 3: ___ ___ ___, ___ ___ ___

Grouping

Individual

You'll Need

◆ Paper
◆ Pencils

Writing Connection

Have students add to their riddles and compile a Math Mystery Number riddle book to share with other fourth graders.

Name That Number!

Students write math riddles and challenge their friends to uncover the math mystery number.

PREPARATION

Write the following math riddle on the chalkboard:

> I am an even number between 40 and 50.
> My two digits add up to 10.
> Who am I?

DIRECTIONS

1. Ask students to solve the riddle. Then ask for a volunteer to explain how he or she solved it. (*The even numbers between 40 and 50 are 40, 42, 44, 46, 48, and 50. Of those, the only number whose digits add up to 10 is 46.*)

2. Tell students it's their turn to write some riddles for mystery numbers. Give the class some guidelines for the clues in the riddles. They should take advantage of any number concepts they're familiar with: I am a multiple of..., I am a factor of..., I am a prime number..., etc. Students should not limit themselves to two clues. Successive clues should narrow the list of possible answers, until there is only one possible answer.

3. Students can now exchange their riddles with classmates, or take turns reading them aloud for the whole class to try. Remind them that to solve the riddle, they should list all the numbers that fit the first clue. With each clue, they should be able to cross numbers off that list. Students can check each other's work. If a riddle doesn't yield an answer, the reader should explain to the writer why it doesn't work. The writer must then fix the clues.

ASSESSMENT

Use the kinds and complexity of clues, and the ability to find an answer, to assess students' familiarity with number concepts.

The United States of Addition

Which state is worth the most points? Students will find out in this addition activity.

PREPARATION

Write the letter-to-number chart on the chalkboard. Display a map of the United States.

DIRECTIONS

1. Explain to students that you've written a list of alphabet point values on the board. They can use the list to add the number of points of all the letters in a word. For example, for the word MATH, M = 13, A = 1, T = 20, and H = 8. 13 + 1 + 20 + 8 = 42. Therefore, the word MATH is worth 42 points. Have students practice by finding the point values of other school subjects.

2. Ask students which state name they think is worth the most points. Record their guesses on the chalkboard. Keep a tally of how many students vote for each state.

3. Divide students into small groups. Assign several states to each group, until all 50 states have been assigned. Have groups add up the point totals for the state names they've been given. Ask each group to report their state with the highest point total. Did anyone correctly predict the "winning" state—Massachusetts?

 ASSESSMENT

Answers: AL = 31, AK = 45, AZ = 84, AR = 84, CA = 88, CO = 83, CT = 127, DE = 68, FL = 65, GA = 62, HI = 51, ID = 37, IL = 99, IN = 52, IA = 48, KS = 65, KY = 110, LA = 101, ME = 42, MD = 88, MA = 168, MI = 64, MN = 110, MS = 157, MO = 123, MT = 78, NE = 71, NV = 47, NH = 139, NJ = 124, NM = 111, NY = 111, NC = 148, ND = 127, OH = 47, OK = 76, OR = 74, PA = 152, RI = 109, SC = 156, SD = 135, TN = 106, TX = 69, UT = 50, VT = 107, VA = 89, WA = 130, WV = 156, WI = 125, WY = 106. Students can rework the additions or use calculators to double-check the calculations of the other members in their group.

 EXTENSION

Have students make a tally chart showing which letters appeared most often and which appeared least often in state names.

Grouping

Small groups

You'll Need

◆ United States map
◆ Paper
◆ Pencils
◆ Calculators (optional)

LETTER-TO-NUMBER CHART

A = 1	N = 14
B = 2	O = 15
C = 3	P = 16
D = 4	Q = 17
E = 5	R = 18
F = 6	S = 19
G = 7	T = 20
H = 8	U = 21
I = 9	V = 22
J = 10	W = 23
K = 11	X = 24
L = 12	Y = 25
M = 13	Z = 26

Touchdown Totals

Students will have "sum" fun with this football-theme game.

Grouping

Whole class

You'll Need

◆ Clock or stopwatch

FOOTBALL SCORES

2 points—safety

3 points—field goal

6 points—touchdown

7 points—touchdown with extra point

Teaching Tip

A referee with a calculator can quickly check each team's combinations.

Writing Connection

Have students summarize the scoring system in another sport, such as soccer, tennis, golf, basketball, softball, baseball, etc.

PREPARATION

On the chalkboard, write a list of football point totals and different scoring combinations to reach each total, as shown on the list below.

DIRECTIONS

1. Explain to students that they'll be playing a football game. The object of the game is to come up with the most scoring combinations. Divide the class into two teams. Let the teams pick names for themselves.

2. Review the game rules. Explain that you will call out a point total. The teams will then have two minutes to come up with as many different scoring combinations as they can, using only the football scoring numbers 2, 3, 6, and 7. For example, if you call the point total of 20, one way to get that score would be two touchdowns with extra points and two field goals—7 + 7 + 3 + 3.

3. Call a number of total points. Numbers you can use include 11, 12, 15, 18, 24, 27, 36. When time is up, each team will report the combinations they found. You or the students should write the combinations on the chalkboard. The team with the most different combinations scores a touchdown and receives 7 points. Keep a running tally of the score on the chalkboard.

4. Begin play again by saying a new point total. You can play a timed game, or set a point limit, such as ending when one team reaches 28 points.

ASSESSMENT

You may want to have individual team members record combinations. They can then each give one, until the team has exhausted all its different combinations.

▶▶▶ EXTENSION

During football season, bring in the sports section of the newspaper. Have students look at the football box scores to see how the scoring added up.

Toni's Take-Away

Subtraction action is needed to make sure customers take away the correct change from this take-out restaurant.

DIRECTIONS

1. Tell your students that it's Marty's first day working at Toni's Take-Away, a popular take-out restaurant. It's lunchtime, and a big line is forming. Those customers are hungry! Marty needs to make sure everyone gets the correct change. And he needs a lot of help.

2. Distribute reproducible page 16 and ask students to look at the orders for each customer in line. Have students do some quick estimation: About how much was spent? About how much change will each customer get? Which customer do they think will get the most change? Who should get the least?

3. Now ask students to find the amount of money each customer spent and the amount of change each should get. Remind students that as they add and subtract amounts of money, they need to be careful to align the decimal points. Also suggest that they be on the lookout for customers ordering more than one of a particular item. For example, to find out how much 2 Toni-Roni pizzas cost, they can use repeated addition or multiplication.

ASSESSMENT

Answers: 1. $.10 **2**. $6.14 **3**. $13.78 **4**. $9.50 **5**. $25.99. If students have incorrect answers, check to see that they recorded the addition and subtraction problems correctly, and that they regrouped when subtracting from zeros.

✦✦✦ VARIATION

Using the menu from Toni's Take-Away and some play money, have students practice making transactions. Students should take turns being customer and cashier.

Grouping

Individual

You'll Need

For each student:

◆ **Toni's Take-Away (reproducible page 16)**

◆ Pencil

Writing Connection

Have students pretend to be Marty after his first day at work and write a diary entry. They should tell what kinds of problems they had and what different types of math they used during the day.

Name _____

Toni's Take-Away

Toni

MENU

CLAMBURGER . . . . $ 2.15	WRENCH FRIES . . . . $ 1.29
ICE-COLD DOG . . . . $ 1.59	NICE CREAM. . . . . $ .79
TONI-RONI PIZZA . . . . . . $ 3.79	GOATMEAL COOKIES . . . . . $ .65
CHICKEN FINGERS . . . . . . $ 4.50	JOKA-COLA . . . . $ 1.05
SAND SANDWICH. . . . . . . $ 3.20	BELLY-ACHE SHAKE. . . . . . $ 1.99
ROCKO'S TACO . . . . $ 1.39	WETTER WATER . . . . $ .88

1. ORDERED:
SAND SANDWICH
GOATMEAL COOKIES
JOKA-COLA

PAYING WITH: $5.00
CHANGE:

2. ORDERED:
ICE-COLD DOG
ROCKO'S TACO
WETTER WATER

PAYING WITH: $10.00
CHANGE:

3. ORDERED:
CLAMBURGER
WRENCH FRIES
NICE CREAM
BELLY-ACHE SHAKE

PAYING WITH: $20.00
CHANGE:

4. ORDERED:
2 TONI-RONI PIZZAS
ROCKO'S TACO
GOATMEAL COOKIES
WETTER WATER

PAYING WITH: $20.00
CHANGE:

5. ORDERED:
3 CHICKEN FINGERS
2 ICE-COLD DOGS
WRENCH FRIES
NICE CREAM
5 JOKA-COLAS

PAYING WITH: $50.00
CHANGE:

50+ Super-Fun Math Activities: Grade 4 © 2010 by Scholastic Inc.

The Human Clock

Invite students to "walk around the clock" as they review the basics of telling time.

PREPARATION

In large letters, use markers to write HOUR HAND on one piece of paper and MINUTE HAND on another. Then label sheets of paper with the numbers 1 through 12.

DIRECTIONS

1. Explain to students that they will be making a "human clock." Ask for volunteers—one to be the hour hand, one to be the minute hand, and 12 to be each of the numbers on a clockface.

2. Have the 12 number students sit in a large circle, each holding up their number, to represent a clockface. Tell the hour hand and minute hand that they are to stand where the hand they are representing would point, as you say a time. For example, if you say 3 o'clock, the minute hand should stand in front of the 12, and the hour hand should stand in front of the 3.

3. Ask the hands to move to a variety of times—noon, times on the quarter-hour or half-hour, the time school begins, and so on. (Every few "times," let other students be the clock hands.)

4. You can use the human clock to review different ways to express the same time, such as 3:30 or half-past three; 5:45 or quarter to six; 8:15 or quarter past eight.

ASSESSMENT

Use an actual or play clock so students can double-check their accuracy as you say a time.

✛✛✛ VARIATION

Whisper a time to the students playing the hour and minute hands. Have them move into position and have the other students give the correct time.

Grouping

Whole class

You'll Need

◆ Paper
◆ Markers

Writing Connection

Ask students to explain what happens to the hour hand and the minute hand as it gets later in the hour. Students might want to illustrate their explanation with a series of drawings.

You'll Need

- A variety of CDs and tapes with song lengths listed
- Paper
- Pencils

Writing Connection

Ask students to explain other ways they think musicians use math.

Musical Minutes

Students will really tune in to this activity as their favorite songs help them compute time!

PREPARATION

Ask students to bring in favorite CDs and tapes from home.

DIRECTIONS

1. Explain to students that musicians have to make sure the total times of their songs will fit onto a CD or audiotape. Point out that song lengths are usually listed on CDs and audiotapes as minutes:seconds, such as 3:43.

2. Divide the class into small groups. Give each group four or five CDs or audiotapes. Tell the groups that their job is to create one side of a new audiotape of songs. The side is 20 minutes long. They must use at least four songs and there must be 4 seconds of silence between each song. Require students to mix and match songs from their different CDs and audiotapes. You may want to set goals, for example, which group can get the closest to 20 minutes or fit the most songs.

3. To add units of time, remind students first to add the seconds, and then to add the minutes. If they get a total of 60 seconds or more, they must convert the seconds to minutes. For example, adding 3:43 and 2:56, the sum of the seconds is 99. The sum of the minutes is 5. Divide the total seconds by 60. The answer of 1R33 gives an extra minute to add to the total minutes, with 33 remaining seconds. So the total time is 6 minutes 33 seconds (6:33).

4. Have each group read the list of songs and times, and the total time for their side of music.

ASSESSMENT

As each group reports their music and time, have the rest of the class verify that they have remembered to allow 4 seconds between each song and that the computations are correct.

➔➔➔ EXTENSION

Have students add the total times of all the groups' audiotape sides to see if the music would fit on an 80-minute CD. To do this, they will need to convert minutes to hours in the same way they converted seconds to minutes.

Benny's Penny

Students will think this poem is funny, and before they know it, they're working with money!

DIRECTIONS

1. Quickly review penny equivalents for these amounts of money: nickel = 5¢ or 5 pennies, dime = 10¢ or 10 pennies, quarter = 25¢ or 25 pennies, dollar = $1 or 100 pennies. Ask students what they can actually buy for these amounts of money and make a list on the chalkboard. Explain to students that they will read about a character named Benny, who discovered that there wasn't much he could buy with some of these coins!

2. Distribute copies of reproducible page 20 and ask a volunteer to read the poem aloud to the class. Suggest that students circle the different types of money mentioned in the poem.

3. After students complete the activity, discuss their responses. If there is disagreement about any of the answers that involve computation, have volunteers write the problem on the chalkboard and explain how to find the answer.

 **ASSESSMENT**

Answers: 1a. 4 more pennies **b.** 9 more pennies **c.** 24 more pennies **d.** 99 more pennies **2.** 10 dimes **3.** 20 nickels **4.** $1.40 **5.** 60¢ (61¢ if he uses his penny!)

 Grouping

Individual

 You'll Need

For each student:
◆ Benny's Penny (reproducible page 20)
◆ Pencil

 Writing Connection

Have students write their own money poem about Benny.

Name _____

Benny's Penny

Pleased to meet you! My name's Benny.
I went to the store with a shiny penny.
I told the owner I wanted a pickle,
But he said it would cost me a nickel.
So I asked if I could buy a lime.
"Sorry," he said, "that costs a dime."
I asked for an apple, and his temper got shorter.
"Don't you know that costs a quarter?"
I picked up a soda, and he started to holler,
"The price of that bottle is exactly one dollar!"
I didn't have a nickel, dime, quarter, or buck;
It looked like I was out of luck.
How many things can you buy with a penny?
The answer is simple: not too many!

Read the poem. Then answer the questions.

1. How many more pennies would Benny need to buy each item?

   a. a pickle? _____

   b. a lime? _____

   c. an apple? _____

   d. a soda? _____

2. How many dimes would Benny need to buy a soda? _____

3. How many nickels would he need to buy a soda? _____

4. How much money would Benny need to buy all the items (pickle, lime, apple, and soda)?

   _____

5. Benny's mom gives him $2. He goes back to the store to buy all the items. How much

   change should Benny get back? _____

➔➔➔ **On the back of this paper, make a list of all the food items mentioned in the poem that Benny wants to buy. Find out what each of them actually costs at a local grocery store.**

Gold Rush Mountain

Students reach new heights of fun in this board game, as they add and subtract amounts of money.

DIRECTIONS

1. Explain to students that they are about to visit a gold mine at the peak of Gold Rush Mountain. The object of the game is to pick up nuggets worth as much money as possible. They'll need sharp money math skills to get there!

2. Distribute reproducible page 22. Demonstrate how to use the spinner by spinning a paper clip around a pencil placed at the spinner's center. Have students cut out their game playing pieces and place them on the board on START at the bottom of the mountain.

3. Players should spin to see who goes first, with the highest number going first. Players take turns spinning and moving ahead the number of spaces spun.

4. If a player lands in a space with a money amount, that amount is added to the player's total. Players should keep track of their money amounts on a separate sheet of paper. If a player lands in a "penalty" space, he or she must subtract the listed money amount.

5. The first player to reach Hank's Gold Mine gets a bonus of $10. The player to reach Hank's Gold Mine with the highest amount of money is the winner.

ASSESSMENT

Students can check each other's addition and subtraction, with a calculator if you like.

 **EXTENSION**

Have students calculate the highest and lowest amounts of money that could be collected on a trip up the mountain.

Grouping

Pairs or groups of 4

You'll Need

For each pair or group:

◆ **Gold Rush Mountain (reproducible page 22)**
◆ Paper
◆ Pencils
◆ Paper clips

Gold Rush Mountain

Climb Gold Rush Mountain. Who will collect the most money by the time all the players reach Hank's Gold Mine?

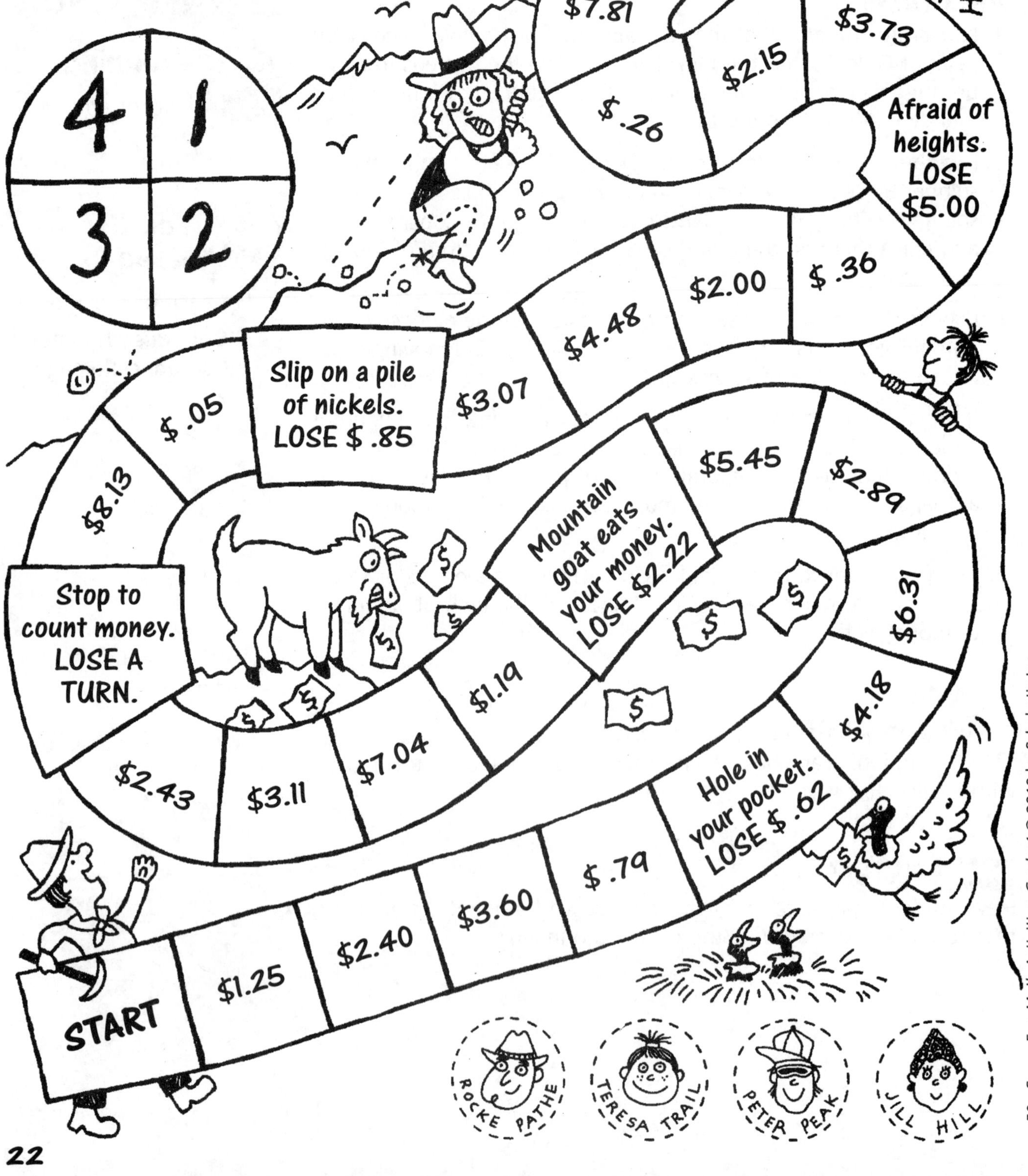

Hank →

$7.81

$2.15

$3.73

$.26

Afraid of heights. LOSE $5.00

$4.48

$2.00

$.36

4 | 1

3 | 2

$.05

Slip on a pile of nickels. LOSE $.85

$3.07

$5.45

$2.89

$8.13

Mountain goat eats your money. LOSE $2.22

$6.31

Stop to count money. LOSE A TURN.

$1.19

$4.18

$2.43

$3.11

$7.04

Hole in your pocket. LOSE $.62

$.79

$3.60

$2.40

$1.25

START

50+ Super-Fun Math Activities: Grade 4 © 2010 by Scholastic Inc.

ROCKE PATHE

TERESA TRAIL

PETER PEAK

JILL HILL

22

Quick Six

Students practice multiplication with the roll of a number cube.

DIRECTIONS

1. Explain to students that they will be playing a multiplication game called Quick Six. Ask each student to write the following numbers on a piece of paper: 1, 2, 3, 4, 5, 6, 8, 9, 10, 12, 15, 16, 18, 20, 24, 25, 30, and 36. These will be multiplication products they're looking for as they play the game.

2. Ask students to form pairs, or assign partners. Distribute the number cubes. Students can roll one number cube each to decide who goes first, with the larger number going first.

3. The first player rolls both number cubes and states a multiplication fact based on the numbers rolled. (For example, if a player rolls a 2 and a 5, he or she should say: 2 times 5 equals 10.) On that player's own piece of paper, that product is crossed out. If the player rolls a product that is already crossed out, it becomes the other player's turn.

4. Players verify each other's multiplication problems. If one player catches a mistake, he or she can cross out the product. The winner is the first player to cross out all the numbers.

 Grouping

Pairs

 You'll Need

For each pair:
◆ 2 number cubes labeled 1–6
◆ Paper
◆ Pencils

ASSESSMENT

Circulate and listen as students say the multiplication facts. Pairs might make up their own sets of flash cards, with correct answers on the back, if they need additional practice.

➔➔➔ EXTENSION

To practice higher multiplication facts, through 12 x 12, students can roll two pairs of number cubes. They add the numbers showing on each pair of cubes and then multiply the two sums.

Mall-tiplication

Mall aboard! Students practice multiplication skills as they go on a shopping spree in this board game!

Grouping

Small groups

You'll Need

For each group:

◆ Mall-tiplication (reproducible page 25)

◆ Paper

◆ Pencils

◆ Paper clips

Writing Connection

Have students keep a detailed list of how many of each item they get. They can use the information to make up and exchange addition and subtraction word problems.

DIRECTIONS

1. Students have all won shopping sprees to the Mall-tiplication Mall. The object of the game is to collect as many items in the mall as possible. To do this, they will need multiplication, addition, and a little luck!

2. Divide the class into small groups. Demonstrate how to make a spinner, by spinning a paper clip around the tip of a pencil. Then distribute the Mall-tiplication reproducible and a paper clip to each group. Have students cut out the game pieces and place them on the board at the Mall Entrance.

3. To begin the game, the player with the highest spin on the outside number circle goes first, and play moves to the left. Players spin twice on each turn. On the first spin, players use the inner set of numbers (1–4) to move forward. When a player lands on a store space, he or she spins again and uses the outer set of numbers (1–9) to multiply the number in the store space. That's the number of items to collect on that turn.

4. At each turn, players add the product of the multiplication problem to their score. Students can keep track of their scores on a separate sheet of paper.

   The first player to reach the Mall Exit gets a bonus of 200 items. The player to reach the Mall Exit with the most items is the winner.

ASSESSMENT

Observe that students are regrouping correctly when they multiply 2-digit numbers.

Mall-tiplication

MALL ENTRANCE

Sneakers **7**

Candies **10**

CDs **5**

Pets **8**

Left bag at Food Court. SUBTRACT **5** items

Bikes **12**

Hats **2**

Comic Books **11**

Stuffed Animals **3**

Hot Dogs **4**

Stopped at Arcade. LOSE A TURN

Radios **15**

Baseball Cards **9**

Skates **13**

Shopping bag broke! SUBTRACT **50** items

TVs **1**

Basketballs **14**

Paperbacks **6**

Kid brother wants to SHARE! SUBTRACT **100** items

Video Games **16**

Sunglasses **19**

Watches **23**

MALL EXIT

 WENDY SPENDER

 DOLLAR BILL

 PENNY NICHOLS

 SONNY MONEY

Math Showdown

This game will "suit" students just fine. Computation practice is in the cards!

Grouping

Pairs

You'll Need

For each pair:

◆ Deck of playing cards

◆ Paper

◆ Pencils

SCORES AND OPERATIONS

Jack and Queen = 11

King and Ace = 12

Club means add

Spade means subtract

Diamond means multiply

Heart means multiply product by 10

PREPARATION

On the chalkboard, write the scores and operations from the chart.

DIRECTIONS

1. Tell students they're about to play a card game called Math Showdown. To win, they'll have to collect the most points. Divide the class into pairs and give each pair a deck of cards.

2. One player in each pair deals the cards facedown until both players have half the deck (as in the game War). To play, players flip over their top card simultaneously. Each player uses the numbers on both cards, and the suit of his or her own card. The suit indicates which mathematical operation he or she must perform using the two numbers. For example: Player 1 turns the 4 of diamonds. Player 2 turns the 6 of spades. Since Player 1's suit is diamonds, Player 1 multiplies 4 x 6. Player 2 uses the same two numbers, but subtracts 6 – 4. If a player's suit is hearts, he or she must multiply the product of the two numbers by 10.

3. If a face card is turned, players should use the numbers indicated in the chart. When both players have played, the turned cards are placed in a discard pile. The players then flip and play again.

4. Each correct answer scores 1 point. If a player gives an incorrect answer or performs the wrong operation, he or she gets no points. Players should tally their scores on separate paper. You can set a time or point limit on the game, or students can play until they've gone through their stack of cards once.

ASSESSMENT

Students should check each other's math, paying attention to whether their opponent is performing the correct operation.

➔➔➔ EXTENSION

Organize a round-robin Math Showdown tournament in your class. Winners in each pair play other winners until an ultimate showdown champion is declared!

Remainder Road Race

Students become race car drivers and use division to reach the finish line in this fast-paced board game.

DIRECTIONS

1. To get ready to play this race car game, review division with remainders. For example, dividing 57 by 8 yields a quotient of 7 and a remainder of 1. Give some other examples and be sure students are comfortable expressing quotients and remainders.

2. Distribute reproducible page 28. Explain to students that they will be playing a game called the Remainder Road Race—and they are the race car drivers! The object is to be the first race car driver to cross the finish line. They'll need to divide and use remainders to get there.

3. Demonstrate how to use the game board spinner. Spin a paper clip around the tip of a pencil placed at the spinner's center. Then divide students into small groups and distribute a game board and paper clip to each group.

4. Students should spin to decide who will go first, with the highest number going first. Play proceeds to the left. Each player takes his or her turn at the starting line and uses the number 19 to begin play.

5. After a player spins, he or she divides the number in the board space by the number on the spinner. When the player finishes the division problem, he or she moves forward the same number of spaces as the REMAINDER of the problem. For example, if a player is on 19 at the starting line and spins ÷ 8, the answer is 2 with a remainder of 3. The player moves ahead 3 spaces. If the problem has no remainder, the player cannot move until his or her next turn.

6. After each group has a winner, discuss the game. Could strategy be used, or was the winner determined by luck? Could a calculator be used to play the game? Why or why not?

ASSESSMENT

Students can check the math of players in their group and make sure they are using the remainder to move forward.

Grouping

Small groups

You'll Need

For each group:

◆ **Remainder Road Race (reproducible page 28)**
◆ Paper
◆ Pencils
◆ Paper clips

Writing Connection

Ask students to analyze how they moved ahead on the game board and then explain what they would need to reach the finish line the fastest. Would spinning the highest or lowest number always help?

Remainder Road Race

Spinner: ÷ 9, ÷ 2, ÷ 3, ÷ 4, ÷ 5, ÷ 6, ÷ 7, ÷ 8

START

103 71 19

47 762

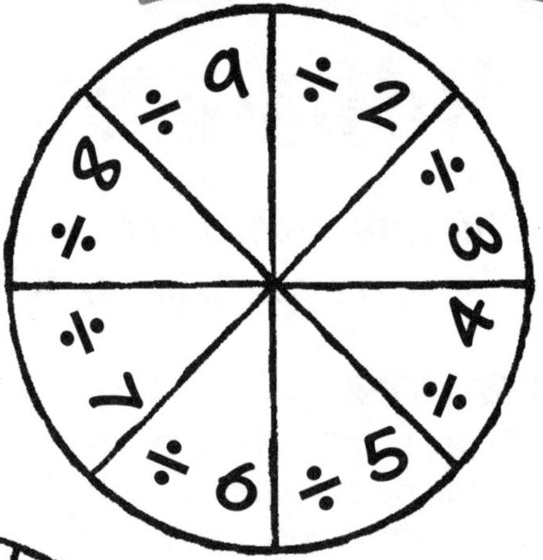

12

35

907 373

755 755

28 40

730

580

302 11

22

54

77 64 14 92 151 99

29

10 50 100 77

199 999

18

FINISH

RAY RACER RHODA MOTOR TYRONE TIRE BRENDA BRAKES

Divide the Cake!

A little computation can help students discover the day of the week on which they were born!

DIRECTIONS

1. Students will undoubtedly know their birth dates. But how many know the day of the week they were born? Tell students that with a little "mathe-magic," they can figure it out.

2. Distribute reproducible page 30 and have students follow the directions to reveal the day of the week on which they were born. They can also compute to see if they share a birth day with any other members of their family.

3. When students are finished, discuss the results. Was any day more common than the others?

▸▸▸ EXTENSION

Have students graph the results of this activity, to show days of the week and number of students born on each day.

Grouping

Individual

You'll Need

For each student:

◆ **Divide the Cake! (reproducible page 30)**

◆ Pencils

Teaching Tip

Make sure students write only the final answer in each step. You may want to ask them to circle that number, to make it stand out. Pay special attention to step 4, to make sure they've dropped the remainder, and to step 6, to make sure they write the remainder.

Divide the Cake!

CHART 1	
January	1
February	4
March	4
April	0
May	2
June	5
July	0
August	3
September	6
October	1
November	4
December	6

CHART 2	
Sunday	1
Monday	2
Tuesday	3
Wednesday	4
Thursday	5
Friday	6
Saturday	0

Follow these directions carefully and you'll discover the day of the month you were born!

1. Look at Chart 1 and find the month you were born. Write the number next to that month. (**Important**: If you were born in a leap year, write 0 if you were born in January and 3 if you were born in February.) _____

2. Write the number for the day of the month you were born. _____

3. Write the last two digits of the year you were born. _____

4. Divide the number in step 3 by 4. If there is a remainder, ignore it. Write the quotient you get. _____

5. Add all of the numbers from steps 1–4. Write the sum. _____

6. Divide the sum from step 5 by 7. Write the remainder. _____

7. Now use Chart 2. Look up the number you got in step 6. That's the day of the week you were born! _____

➤➤➤ **Were you born on the same day of the week as anyone else in your family? Use their birth dates and follow steps 1–7 to find out!**

The Unit Price Is Right!

Students will be smarter shoppers when they learn to compute unit price.

DIRECTIONS

1. Pose this question to students:

   There are 2 boxes of cookies. A 20-ounce box costs $1.60, and a 30-ounce box costs $2.10. Which is a better deal?

   Tell them that knowing about unit prices can help them figure this out.

2. Explain that a unit price tells how much one unit of an item costs. (A unit is the measurement used for an item, such as ounces or liters.) The lower the unit price, the better the deal.

3. Show students how to compute the unit price by dividing the price of the item by the number of units (the size of the item). For example, for the smaller box of cookies, the unit price would be $1.60 ÷ 20 ounces, or $.08 per ounce. For the larger box, it would be $2.10 ÷ 30, or $.07 per ounce. So the larger box is the better deal.

4. Divide the class into small groups. Give each group some supermarket circulars. Ask each group to find the unit price of at least two similar items. You may want to assign a shopping list of types of items, such as cereal, pretzels, a can of soup, milk. Ask students to keep track of the store each ad is for. As they do the computation, tell students always to round the unit price to the nearest cent.

5. Have each group share their results with the class. Did any store have consistently lower unit prices? How did sale prices affect unit prices? You might make a class chart listing stores and unit prices for the grocery items on the groups' shopping list.

ASSESSMENT
Make sure students are dividing the cost by the size, not vice versa.

▶▶▶ EXTENSION
Have students make a list of five items and find the unit prices in a local grocery store. Many stores list the unit prices right on the shelves.

Grouping

Small groups

You'll Need

◆ Supermarket circulars and newspaper supermarket ads
◆ Calculators (optional)

Teaching Tip

If calculators are available, students will be able to find unit prices more quickly.

Writing Connection

Ask students to imagine they're buying a box of cereal. Ask them to explain what things they would consider besides the unit price.

Name _____

Problems and More

Put on your thinking cap to solve these problems.

1. MAGIC SQUARE

Using the numbers 1 to 9, fill in the squares so the rows across, down, and diagonally all add up to 15.

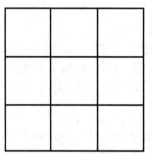

2. POCKET CHANGE

I have 19 coins in my pocket. I have twice as many dimes as nickels, three more pennies than nickels, and one more dime than the number of pennies. My coins add up to $1.07. How many of each coin do I have?

_____ dimes

_____ nickels

_____ pennies

3. CONNECT THE DOTS

Can you connect all of the dots with four straight lines? Here's the catch: You can't lift your pencil!

4. A SNEAKY PUZZLE

Something is hiding under your bed! To find out what it is, do this problem on a calculator:

5,000 + 45,842 + 2,203.

Turn the calculator upside down to reveal the answer.

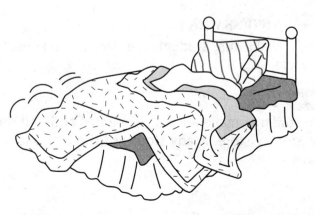

50+ Super-Fun Math Activities: Grade 4 © 2010 by Scholastic Inc.

Answers on page 64.

Problems and More

5. LETTERS IN A LINE

Fill in the next three letters in this pattern: O, T, T, F, F, S, S, ___, ___, ___

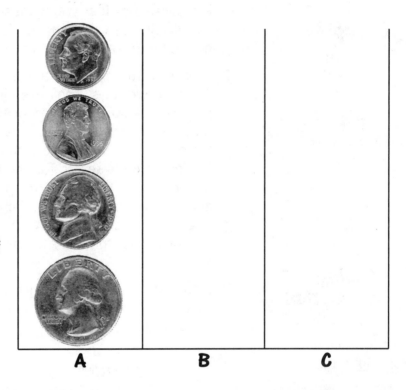

6. COIN COLUMNS

Can you move all of the coins from column A to column C? You can move only the top coin in a column. And you can't put a larger-size coin on top of a smaller-size coin.

A   B   C

7. AN ODD RIDDLE

Question: How can you make "seven" even? _____

8. TRICKY TRIANGLES

How many triangles can you find in the design below?

9. PICK-UP STICKS

Move only one of the toothpicks to make this equation true:

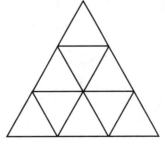

50+ Super-Fun Math Activities: Grade 4 © 2010 by Scholastic Inc.

Shape Safari

When students enter the geometry jungle, they'll track down elusive polygons.

Grouping

Individual

You'll Need

◆ Paper
◆ Pencils

Writing Connection

Have students choose one of the shapes they found and write a short description of it. The description should help someone who has never heard of this shape be able to identify it.

DIRECTIONS

1. Review shapes that you want students to look for. These might include circle, oval, triangle, square, rectangle, trapezoid, pentagon, hexagon, octagon.

2. Explain to students that they'll be going on a Shape Safari over the next two days. Their mission is to track down as many polygons as possible! Introduce them to some of the wild shapes they might encounter—the soaring circle, the squawking square, the roaring rectangle, the awful oval, and the timid triangle. Students should search for and keep a list all of the polygons they can find. They can look in the school, along the way home, and at home. A door might be a rectangle; a basketball hoop might be a circle; an arrow on a sign might contain a triangle. On their lists, students should write each shape and where it was located.

3. Have each student report her or his results. Who found the most shapes? Who had the widest variety of shapes? What was the rarest shape found?

ASSESSMENT

Students' lists of real-world objects should accurately represent geometric shapes.

✛✛✛ VARIATION

Include solid shapes, such as cubes, cylinders, spheres, rectangular prisms, etc., in the activity.

➔➔➔ EXTENSION

Invite students to explore these books on shapes in architecture: *The Village of Round and Square Houses* by Ann Grifalconi; David Macaulay's *Cathedral, City, Pyramid, Underground, Castle,* or *Unbuilding.*

Get-in-Shape Equations

How do you "add" shapes? In this geometry activity, triangle + triangle = hexagon.

DIRECTIONS

1. Draw each of the polygons from the reproducible—triangle, rectangle, pentagon, hexagon, heptagon, octagon, nonagon, decagon, and dodecagon—on the chalkboard. Review the shapes students are familiar with and ask students to tell the number of sides on each. Then introduce the shapes that are new to students.

2. Distribute reproducible page 36 to each student. Ask students to cut out each polygon and math symbol (+, −, x, ÷, =) from the sheet.

3. Have students form equations based on the number of sides on each polygon. For example: octagon − triangle = pentagon; hexagon + triangle − rectangle = pentagon. Make sure they realize that they can use equations with more than two terms. Challenge students to manipulate their shapes to create as many different equations as possible. They should record a list of their equations on a separate sheet of paper.

4. After 10 or 15 minutes, have students share their equations. Who had the most equations? Who had the longest equation?

ASSESSMENT
Note which students were able to use all operations to invent equations. On longer equations, make sure students followed the proper order of operations.

➡➡➡ EXTENSION
Have students create and name interesting new shapes of their own. They can use their own shapes to write equations.

Grouping

Individual

You'll Need

For each student:

◆ **Get-in-Shape Equations (reproducible page 36)**
◆ Scissors
◆ Paper
◆ Pencil

Get-in-Shape Equations

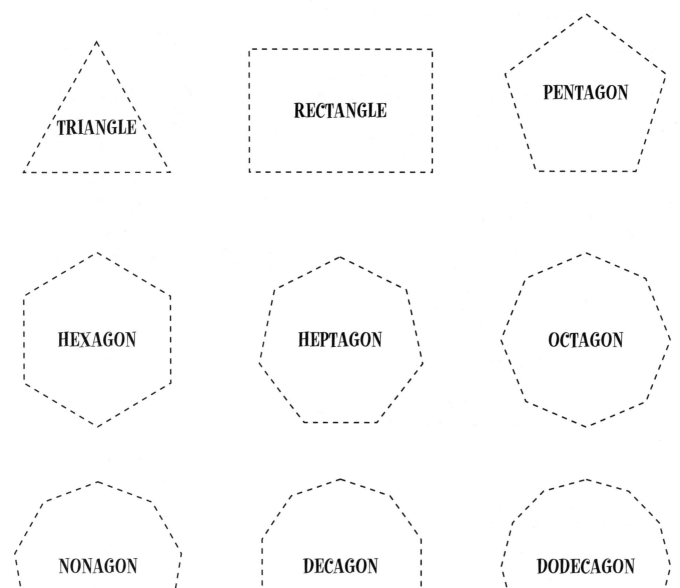

TRIANGLE

RECTANGLE

PENTAGON

HEXAGON

HEPTAGON

OCTAGON

NONAGON

DECAGON

DODECAGON

50+ Super-Fun Math Activities: Grade 4 © 2010 by Scholastic Inc.

Coordinate Corner

**By plotting coordinate points,
students will reveal a secret message.**

DIRECTIONS

1. Display a coordinate grid on the chalkboard or overhead projector. Point out that the x-axis (the horizontal line) and the y-axis (the vertical line) are actually two intersecting number lines.

2. Explain a coordinate point—a point on the grid where two lines meet and cross. The location of a coordinate point can be identified by using ordered pairs, such as (2,5). The ordered pair (2,5) is located by moving 2 spaces to the right on the x-axis, and 5 spaces up on the y-axis, and drawing a coordinate point. This is called plotting a point. If students have worked with variables, you may want to show that an ordered pair can be written as (x,y). This may help them understand which axis to move along for each number.

3. Distribute reproducible page 38 and tell students they'll practice plotting points to reveal a secret message. "Point" out the x- and y-axes and the numbers on them.

4. When students are finished plotting all the listed points, ask them to connect the points in the order they are listed to reveal a secret message.

ASSESSMENT

If students plot the points correctly, they should reveal the secret message HI, written in large block letters.

▸▸▸ EXTENSION

Distribute blank coordinate grids and have students make simple drawings or messages on them. Have students list all the ordered pairs, in order, on a separate sheet. They can exchange sheets with a partner and try to duplicate their partner's drawing or message.

✦✦✦ VARIATION

Lines of latitude and longitude on a map create a type of coordinate grid. Have students find these lines on a map, in a social studies text, for example, and see if they can locate a given city by degrees of latitude and longitude.

Grouping
Individual

You'll Need

For each student:
- **Coordinate Corner (reproducible page 38)**
- Pencil

Name _____

Coordinate Corner

Plot the following ordered pairs. Then connect them in the order they're given, and you'll reveal a secret message!

Connect these first.

(1,12) (1,4) (3,4) (3,7) (5,7) (5,4) (7,4) (7,12) (5,12) (5,9) (3,9) (3,12) (1,12)

Now connect these.

(9,12) (9,10) (11,10) (11,6) (9,6) (9,4) (15,4) (15,6) (13,6) (13,10) (15,10) (15,12) (9,12)

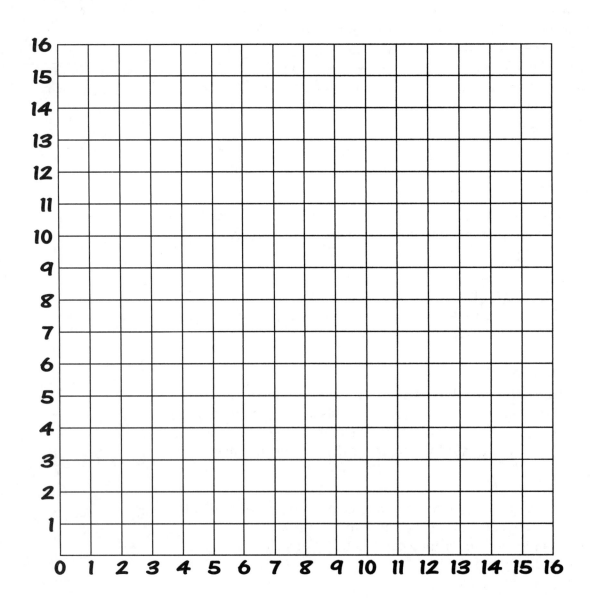

50+ Super-Fun Math Activities: Grade 4 © 2010 by Scholastic Inc.

The Great Skate Hunt

Students will be "on a roll" with map skills and directions as they help Willy Wheeler find his missing skateboard.

DIRECTIONS

1. Explain to students that Willy Wheeler and his sister Wendy are visiting Scott's Skate School. Wendy has hidden Willy's skateboard, but she gave him directions that will lead him to it.

2. Distribute reproducible page 40 and rulers. Point out Wendy's list of directions, the map scale, and the compass that shows directions on the map. If necessary, review compass points with your class, beginning with the cardinal points—north, east, south, and west—and continuing to northeast, southeast, southwest, and northwest. Also review the map distance scale. On the Skate School map, 1 centimeter stands for 10 meters. So if Willy is told to walk 30 meters, on the map he would move 3 centimeters.

3. Ask students to use the list of directions to find the skateboard. They should begin where Willy is standing, use the stars as they measure, and draw lines on the map as they follow each consecutive direction. For each of Wendy's directions, students must pay attention to a number and a compass direction. For example, if Wendy's list says 50m SE, Willy should walk 50 meters (5 cm) to the southeast.

ASSESSMENT
Make sure that students' lines on their maps go from one star to another at each landmark and that they are using the compass correctly. **Answer:** The skateboard is hidden at the Trash Dash.

✦✦✦ VARIATION
Have students "hide" Willy's skateboard in another spot and make their own list of directions for him to find it. Students can exchange lists and see if they can follow one another's directions correctly.

➔➔➔ EXTENSION
Ask students to figure out the total distance of Willy's trip around the Skate School. Then ask them to measure to find out the distance if Willy had gone right to the place where his board was hidden.

Grouping
Individual

You'll Need

For each student:
◆ **The Great Skate Hunt (reproducible page 40)**
◆ Metric ruler
◆ Crayons or pencils

The Great Skate Hunt

Distance Scale

1 cm = 10 meters

DIRECTIONS

1. 50 m SE
2. 90 m N
3. 70 m NE
4. 80 m SE
5. 60 m S
6. 80 m W
7. 40 m NW
8. 40 m E

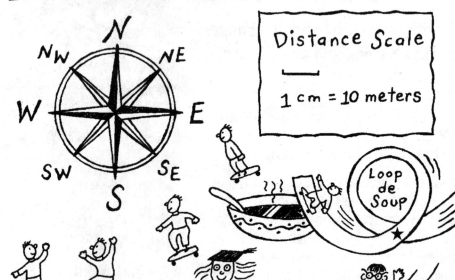

Loop de Soup

Board of Education

SCOTT'S SKATE SCHOOL

Jump Rope Jump

Here!

Rolling Roll Call

Willy Wheeler

Trash Dash

Start Here!

Skate Date

Gramp's Ramp

Rock 'n' Roll

50+ Super-Fun Math Activities: Grade 4 © 2010 by Scholastic Inc.

Fruit and Fractions

Here's a "cool" fruit salad recipe that adds up to fraction practice.

PREPARATION

If you are going to prepare the fruit salad in class, see the recipe for preparation details. Adjust the ingredients to your class size.

DIRECTIONS

1. Explain to students that you are giving them a recipe they can try at home. The recipe makes enough Rootin' Tootin' Fruit Salad to serve 3 people. Ask students how they would determine the amount of ingredients to serve 6 people. They may suggest adding, or multiplying by 2.

2. Review with students how to add fractions with like denominators by adding the numerators. Also review that when the numerator is equal to the denominator (such as the sum of ½ + ½), the fraction equals 1 (²⁄₂ = 1). Depending on students' experience with fractions, you may want them to reduce each fraction to lowest terms when possible (²⁄₄ = ½).

3. Distribute reproducible page 42 and have students double the recipe, filling in the new ingredient amounts on the blanks. Review the results as a class. If students will make the recipe in class, distribute the ingredients and utensils and have students make the fruit salad.

 ASSESSMENT

Answers: ²⁄₃ pound seedless grapes, ²⁄₄ or ½ cup blueberries, 1 banana, ²⁄₈ or ¼ cup orange juice, 2 tablespoons sugar, 4 teaspoons cornstarch. Watch for a common error: students add both the numerator and denominator when adding fractions.

▶▶▶ EXTENSION

Ask students what they could do to find how much of each ingredient they would need for 9 people. For 12 people? Challenge them to use repeated addition to find the new amounts.

✦✦✦ VARIATION

This recipe can also be used to practice fraction multiplication. Simply multiply each fraction by 2 for six servings, by 3 for nine servings, or by 4 for twelve servings.

 Grouping

Individual

Small groups or whole class to make the recipe

You'll Need

◆ **Fruit and Fractions (reproducible page 42),** one copy for each student

◆ Optional (to make the recipe): seedless grapes, blueberries, bananas, apples, orange juice, sugar, cornstarch, 2 mixing bowls, measuring spoons, measuring cups, spoon, knife

 Writing Connection

Where else besides recipes do students encounter fractions? Ask them to make a list.

Fruit and Fractions

This cool fruit salad serves 3 people. Figure out the amount of each ingredient you'll need to serve 6 people.

ROOTIN' TOOTIN' FRUIT SALAD RECIPE

Ingredient	To Serve 3 People:	To Serve 6 People:
seedless grapes	$\frac{1}{3}$ pound	_____
blueberries	$\frac{1}{4}$ cup	_____
banana	$\frac{1}{2}$	_____
orange juice	$\frac{1}{8}$ cup	_____
sugar	1 tablespoon	_____
cornstarch	2 teaspoons	_____

INSTRUCTIONS

1. Remove the grapes from the stem and wash them carefully. Take out any bruised grapes.

2. Wash the blueberries carefully, removing any bruised ones.

3. Place the grapes and blueberries in a large bowl.

4. Slice the banana into 1-inch chunks and add the slices to the bowl.

5. In a separate bowl, mix together the orange juice, sugar, and cornstarch. Pour the mixture over your salad. This will keep the fruit fresh.

50+ Super-Fun Math Activities: Grade 4 © 2010 by Scholastic Inc.

Farm-Fresh Fractions

**Old MacDonald had a farm. On that farm,
he had some fractions. E-I-E-I-O!**

DIRECTIONS

1. Review that a fraction represents part of a whole or group. For a group, the denominator represents the total number or the whole group. The numerator represents a given number or portion of those objects. Use the number of students in your classroom as an example and ask volunteers to give fractions that represent the number of girls and the number of boys in the class. For example, if there are 25 students and 14 of them are girls, $\frac{14}{25}$ of the class are girls and $\frac{11}{25}$ of the class are boys.

2. Distribute reproducible page 44. The rhyme under each picture instructs students to color in a certain fraction of the objects. Make sure students see the direct relationship between the denominator and the number of animals or people in each problem.

3. When students have finished coloring their fractions, review their work as a class. Ask students to say two fractions for each group: the fraction that represents the colored-in part of the group and the fraction that represents the part of the group that hasn't been colored.

ASSESSMENT

Observe students as they are working to be sure they are coloring in the number indicated by the numerator of each fraction.

➤➤➤ EXTENSION

Ask students to circle $\frac{1}{2}$ of the horses or $\frac{1}{2}$ of the chicks. How would they divide the group of horses or the group of chicks into two equal parts? You can use the illustrations to discuss equivalent fractions: $\frac{1}{2}$ is the same as $\frac{2}{4}$ or $\frac{3}{6}$.

Grouping

Individual

You'll Need

For each student:

◆ **Farm-Fresh Fractions (reproducible page 44)**

◆ Crayons or markers

Writing Connection

Invite students to write their own fraction rhymes and draw pictures based on another setting—the jungle, outer space, the Wild West, etc. Students can exchange their rhymes with classmates.

Farm-Fresh Fractions

Read each rhyme and color in groups of animals or people.

1. Look, a calf! And another calf!
   Won't you please color $\frac{1}{2}$?

2. We've been visited by some birds.
   They'd like it if you'd color $\frac{2}{3}$.

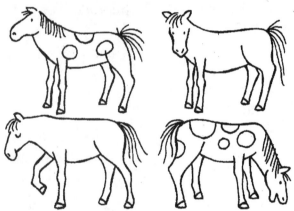

3. It's four times better than just one horse!
   Hey there, pardner, color $\frac{3}{4}$.

4. Here are ducks carrying gifts.
   Help them out. Color $\frac{2}{5}$.

5. All in a row, it's a bunch of chicks.
   They'd be delighted if you'd color $\frac{4}{6}$.

6. It's the farmer's sons, all named Kevin!
   See if you can color $\frac{5}{7}$.

Serving Up Fractions

Students expand their understanding of fractions as they piece together plate puzzles.

PREPARATION

Draw a line down the middle of one paper plate. Label the left and right sides ½. Divide and label a second plate to represent fourths (¼), and a third plate to represent eighths (⅛).

DIRECTIONS

1. Review the use of fractions to divide an object into equivalent parts. Use your prepared plates as examples. If something is divided into two equal parts, each part is ½ of the entire object. If an object is divided into 4 equal parts, each part is ¼. If an object is divided into 8 equal parts, each part is ⅛.

2. Demonstrate how to write equations to show how fractions add up to one whole. On the chalkboard, write these equations: ½ + ½ = 1; ¼ + ¼ + ¼ + ¼ = 1. Ask a volunteer to write an equation to show addition of eighths to make a whole.

3. Distribute paper plates and ask students to divide and label their three plates as you have done—into halves, fourths, and eighths. Have students cut their plates into the various fraction pieces.

4. Ask students to rearrange the fraction pieces to make complete "plates." For example, they could use a half and two fourths. (½ + ¼ + ¼ = 1). Ask them to write an equation for each combination. Challenge students to come up with as many different plate equations as possible!

ASSESSMENT

Possible answers: ½ + ½ = 1; ¼ + ¼ + ¼ + ¼ = 1; ⅛ + ⅛ + ⅛ + ⅛ + ⅛ + ⅛ + ⅛ + ⅛ = 1; ½ + ¼ + ¼ = 1; ½ + ¼ + ⅛ + ⅛ = 1; ½ + ⅛ + ⅛ + ⅛ + ⅛ = 1; ¼ + ⅛ + ⅛ + ⅛ + ⅛ + ⅛ + ⅛ = 1; ¼ + ¼ + ⅛ + ⅛ + ⅛ + ⅛ = 1; ¼ + ¼ + ¼ + ⅛ + ⅛ = 1. Check that students are not simply rewriting the same equation with the fractions in different orders.

▶▶▶ EXTENSION

Repeat the activity, using paper squares instead of circles. By adding a group of sixteenths (1⁄16) to the activity, students will have many more equation possibilities.

Grouping

Individual or small groups

You'll Need

For each student or group:

◆ 3 paper plates
◆ Scissors
◆ Paper
◆ Pencils

A Fraction for Your Thoughts

Pennies can help students conceptualize fractions.

DIRECTIONS

1. Review that a fraction represents a part of a whole. The denominator tells how many parts are in the whole object or group. The numerator tells how many parts of the whole object or group we're looking at.

2. Distribute a cup and 10 pennies to each student. Tell students to put all 10 pennies into their cup, shake them up, and pour them out onto the top of their desk. Ask students how many heads are showing and how they would express this as a fraction of the total number of coins. For example, if a student has 6 heads showing, the fraction of heads is 6/10. Ask what fraction would represent the tails for this trial. *(4/10)*

3. Have students practice writing fractions on their own. They can start with 2 pennies in the cup. For each trial, have them record two fractions: the fraction of heads that came up, and the fraction of tails. Have students increase the total number of coins by 1 on each successive roll.

4. Point out that when the numerator equals the denominator, the fraction is equal to 1. If the numerator is 0, the fraction equals 0.

ASSESSMENT

Be sure students do not reverse the numerator and denominator as they write their fractions. For each roll, the student's two fractions should add up to 1.

✦➔✦➔ EXTENSION

A fraction is also a way to express chance, or probability. For example, when flipping a coin, there are two possible results: heads or tails. The probability of getting heads is 1 out of 2, or ½. Have students experiment with one of their pennies to prove that this is true.

Decimals Are a Hit!

You'll hit a homerun in your class when you use batting averages to introduce reading and comparing decimals.

DIRECTIONS

1. Ask a baseball fan in the class to explain the importance of a batting average. (The number shows how good a hitter a baseball player is.) Explain that a batting average is always expressed as a 3-digit decimal number.

2. Write a batting average on the chalkboard, such as .351. Point out the decimal point and the decimal place values.

.   3   5   1
decimal   tenths   hundredths   thousandths
point

3. Write a second batting average, such as .357, directly beneath the first. If these are two players' batting averages, who is the better hitter? To compare batting averages, students need to align decimal points and compare the digits in the same decimal places, starting at the left of the decimal point. In the example, both numbers have a 3 in the tenths place and a 5 in the hundredths place. In the thousandths place, .357 has a 7 and .351 has 1; so .357 is the greater number and that player has a higher batting average.

4. Distribute reproducible page 48 to each student. Ask students to rank the players from the one with the highest to the one with the lowest batting average. On the blanks next to the averages they should write the numbers 1 to 10, with 1 for the highest average and 10 for the lowest.

 **Grouping**

Individual

 You'll Need

◆ **Decimals Are a Hit! (reproducible page 48),** one copy for each student

◆ Sports section from newspaper (optional)

ASSESSMENT

Answers: 1—Homer Unn; 2—Cal Napkin, Jr.; 3—Babe Ruthless; 4—Cathy Catcher; 5—Greta Play; 6—Thea Ballgame; 7—Mitzi Pitches; 8—Silly Mays; 9—Stella Strikeout; 10—Ken Whiffey, Jr. Observe if students use an organized strategy when they rank the decimal values or whether they work randomly and have to keep changing the order.

➔➔➔ EXTENSION

If the activity is done during baseball season, look through the sports section of a local newspaper. Have students find the batting averages of their favorite players and rank the players.

Decimals Are a Hit!

Rank the players in order from the best to the worst batting average. The player with the highest average should be 1, the player with the lowest average should be 10.

Player	Average	Rank
Babe Ruthless	.342	____
Stella Strikeout	.233	____
Silly Mays	.276	____
Cathy Catcher	.321	____
Ken Whiffey, Jr.	.216	____
Greta Play	.302	____
Homer Unn	.351	____
Mitzi Pitches	.294	____
Cal Napkin, Jr.	.344	____
Thea Ballgame	.296	____

50+ Super-Fun Math Activities: Grade 4 © 2010 by Scholastic Inc.

Decimal Derby

This decimal game is easy: To play it, students just have to say it!

DIRECTIONS

1. Tell students they'll be playing a decimal game. To score, they just have to say decimals! Review decimal place value as needed. Remind students that to say a decimal number, they simply say the number, ignoring the decimal point, and then say the place value of the last digit on the right. For example, .34 is read "thirty-four hundredths." For numbers greater than 1, they should say "and" to represent the decimal point. For example, 3.146 is read as "three and one hundred forty-six thousandths."

2. On the four separate sheets of paper, have each student write the following: decimals of one, two, and three digits; and a number greater than 1 ending in a decimal.

3. Assign pairs and have pairs sit facing each other. Ask players to place their stacks of papers facedown in front in them. Pairs should decide which player "shows" first and which one "talks" first. To play the game, one student holds up his or her first sheet. The other student reads the decimal aloud. If the decimal is read correctly, the talker gets 10 points. Students can tally their scores on separate paper.

4. Students should alternate being the shower and the talker. Play continues until all the sheets have been used. The winner is the student who received more points. To keep the game going, pairs can switch with other pairs and have a whole new set of decimal numbers to read.

ASSESSMENT

Partners should assess each other. Both must agree that the decimal number was said correctly. Make sure students are adding the *-ths* sound to the end of the place value.

✦✦✦ VARIATION

Play the game again, asking students to write the decimal number in words rather than saying it aloud.

Grouping

Pairs

You'll Need

For each student:

◆ 4 sheets of scrap paper
◆ Pencil

Teaching Tip

Adjust the directions to meet students' needs. For example, you may want the largest decimal number to go to the ten thousandths place.

Grouping

Individual

You'll Need

For each student:

◆ Across-and-Down Decimals (reproducible page 51)

◆ Pencil

Across-and-Down Decimals

Students need to look both ways in this crossnumber puzzle—and add decimals while they're at it!

DIRECTIONS

1. Before students begin the crossnumber puzzle, you may want to review how to add decimals. The most important thing for students to remember is to align the decimal points. If one decimal has fewer digits to the right of the decimal point than the other, it is often helpful to add zeros to the end of the shorter number. For example:

INCORRECT   3.4
             + 1.66   →   CORRECT   3.40
                                       + 1.66

When students have aligned the decimal points and added any necessary zeros, they can proceed as if they were adding whole numbers. Remind them to put the decimal point in the sum.

2. Distribute reproducible page 51 to each student. Tell students to complete the crossnumber puzzle as if it were a crossword puzzle. They should give each digit and decimal point its own square.

ASSESSMENT

If students complete all of the decimal addition problems, they should be able to self-check this puzzle. **Answers: Across—A.** 3.7 **C.** 4.38 **E.** .55 **F.** .6 **G.** .9 **J.** .57 **K.** 7.16 **L.** 4.3 **Down—A.** 3.14 **B.** 76.29 **C.** 4.5 **D.** 8.1 **F.** .2704 **H.** 24.3 **I.** 1.7 **J.** .36.

➤➤➤ EXTENSION

Distribute graph paper to your students and challenge them to design their own crossnumber puzzles. Use whatever math skill you wish. Students can exchange puzzles with classmates. If students have trouble inventing their own, they might start with the grid on reproducible page 51.

Across-and-Down Decimals

ACROSS

A. 1.3 + 2.4

C. 2.2 + 2.18

E. .3 + .25

F. .3 + .3

G. .56 + .34

J. .4 + .17

K. 6.93 + .23

L. 1.18 + 3.12

DOWN

A. 1.44 + 1.7

B. 23.11 + 53.18

C. 2.25 + 2.25

D. 6.5 + 1.6

F. .1604 + .11

H. 20.8 + 3.5

I. 1.367 + .333

J. .2 + .16

Grouping

Pairs

You'll Need

◆ Classroom objects such as scissors, pencils, paper clips

Measure Mania!

Do students know their height in bananas? Or CDs? Anything can be a unit of measurement!

DIRECTIONS

1. Explain to students that anything can be used as a unit of measurement—a finger, a shoelace, a book, a pencil—anything! Ask each student to pick a unit to measure a classmate's height. (No rulers allowed!)

2. Divide the class into pairs. Ask students to measure their partners' height, armspan, handspan, and foot length with the unit of measurement they've chosen. Have students record their results. Remind them to label the measurements with the unit they selected. Students might want to name the units they came up with. A shoelace could equal "1 Janice," for example, or "1 fleeber."

3. Have students share their results with the class. Discuss the accuracy of the measurements and the ease someone else would have using their units. Ask students why they think common units (inch, foot, centimeter) and common tools (ruler, meterstick), rather than the units and tools they used in this activity, are the way people usually measure.

ASSESSMENT

Observe whether students are using an accurate method of measurement—marking the end of their measurement unit on their partner and beginning to measure again from that point.

→→→ EXTENSIONS

◆ Have students go around the classroom, measuring the height or length of various items with their units of measurement. What happens if an object is smaller than their unit of measurement? Is it easier to measure large objects with big or small units of measurement?

◆ Pick one unit of measurement. Divide students into groups and have them measure the length and width of different rooms in the school with the same unit of measure. Use the results to make a table with the dimensions of the different rooms.

Measure to the Treasure

Following directions and accurate measurement will help students find a secret spot.

DIRECTIONS:

1. Explain that students will be writing directions and then trying to follow someone else's directions. Assign pairs and tell students that each pair should pick two locations in the school—a starting point and a finishing point. (You may want to limit these locations to indoors, on one floor of the school, or in your classroom). Distribute metersticks or yardsticks.

2. Pairs of students should write a set of directions between the two points, using measurements as part of the directions. The directions should begin by saying exactly where to start and which direction to face. For example: Start at the door of the classroom, facing the chalkboard. The directions should then tell precisely how to get from one spot to the other. For example: Walk 6 meters forward. Turn left and walk 5 more meters.

3. After all the groups have completed their directions, have them sign them and then swap directions with another pair. One student should read the directions aloud, and the pair should follow them together. When they think they've found the secret location, they should check with the pair who wrote the directions to see if they've found the right spot.

4. You may want to set a 5- to 10-minute time limit on following the directions. When all groups have reconvened, discuss the activity. Ask pairs to evaluate how clearly the directions were written and how they might have been presented more clearly.

ASSESSMENT

Each group should check back with the team that gave them the directions. Did they find the correct spot? If not, how could the directions have been better?

 **VARIATION**

Have students do the activity again using a nonstandard unit, such as paces, to write their directions. Discuss how a nonstandard unit affected the results. Was it easier or more difficult to write the directions? to follow them?

 Grouping

Pairs

 You'll Need

For each pair:
◆ Meterstick or yardstick
◆ Paper
◆ Pencil

 Teaching Tip

If you do not have metersticks or yardsticks for each pair, students can make their own using paper or string.

 Writing Connection

Ask students to create a list of times they might need to give or get directions and how measurement labels add to the clarity of directions.

Meatball Measurement!

Which ants will reach the meatballs?
Students must measure curves to find out!

Grouping

Pairs

You'll Need

For each pair:

◆ Meatball Measurement (reproducible page 55)

◆ String, 15 inches long

◆ Scissors

◆ Rulers

◆ Pencils

DIRECTIONS

1. Ask students when they might have to measure nonlinear distances. Students may mention measuring around something, such as a tree trunk. Ask students how they could measure such a distance. Allow several students to give their ideas.

2. Assign pairs and distribute reproducible page 55 and the measuring equipment. Tell students that the ants on the table are hungrily eyeing the meatballs on the floor. The only way to reach the meatballs is to crawl down the strands of spaghetti. All but one of the five spaghetti strands are long enough to reach the meatball underneath. To find out which ones reach—and the one that doesn't—students will have to measure the spaghetti.

3. Ask students how they can use the equipment you've given them to measure each strand of spaghetti. If necessary, show students how to place the end of the piece of string at one end of a spaghetti strand and run the rest of the string along the spaghetti strand, including any curves and loops. One student can place the string, while the partner helps hold it in place.

4. When the curved length is determined, one student can hold the ruler while the partner pulls the string straight and measures it. Students should record the length of each spaghetti strand and then measure the distance from the top of the table to the top of one of the meatballs. Which strands are equal to or longer than this distance?

ASSESSMENT

Here are the lengths of the spaghetti strands, from left to right: 4¼ inches, 6½ inches, 5¼ inches, 6¼ inches, 9¼ inches. The ants Abbie and Arnie won't reach the meatballs.

→→→ EXTENSION

Ask students to compute how much longer Abbie's and Arnie's strands would have to be to reach the meatballs.

Meatball Measurement!

These hungry ants all want a meatball! Record the length of each spaghetti.
Circle the ants who can reach their meatball.

ABBIE   **AKIO**   **ARNIE**   **ARETHA**   **ANTHONY**

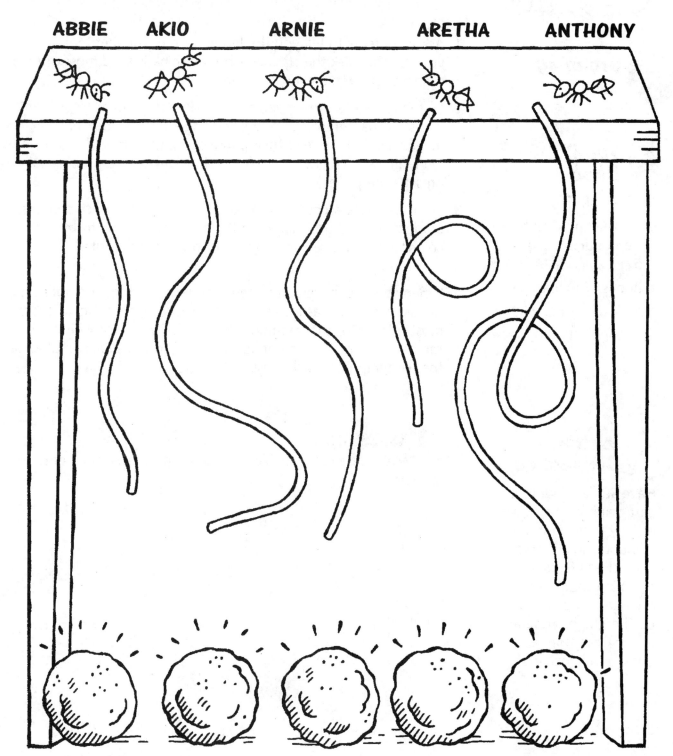

Para-Graph Graphs

Students prowl for vowels in their favorite books to help them build a bar graph!

DIRECTIONS

1. Ask volunteers to tell you the letters of the alphabet that are vowels. Then ask the class which they think is used most often in running text. Have everyone vote.

2. Distribute books or magazines and ask each student to pick out one short paragraph—4 or 5 lines long—from a book or magazine. As they read their paragraphs, they should count how many times each vowel appears. (They can keep a running tally on separate paper.)

3. Next distribute a copy of reproducible page 57 to each student. Students should use their data to construct bar graphs by coloring bars above each vowel up to the number of appearances.

4. When students have completed their work, compare graphs and discuss the results as a class. Ask students which vowel appeared most often. Do students think the graphs would look different if the books were in different languages? Did the subject matter of the paragraph affect the results?

 ASSESSMENT

Make sure students have properly transferred their data to the graphs.

 Grouping

Individual

 You'll Need

For each student:

◆ **Para-Graph Graphs (reproducible page 57)**

◆ Books or magazines

◆ Crayons or markers

◆ Paper

◆ Pencil

 Writing Connection

Have students write a paragraph of their own on any topic. Distribute additional blank graphs and ask students to fill them in based on their own paragraphs. How do the graphs compare to the ones from a book or magazine?

Para-Graph Graphs

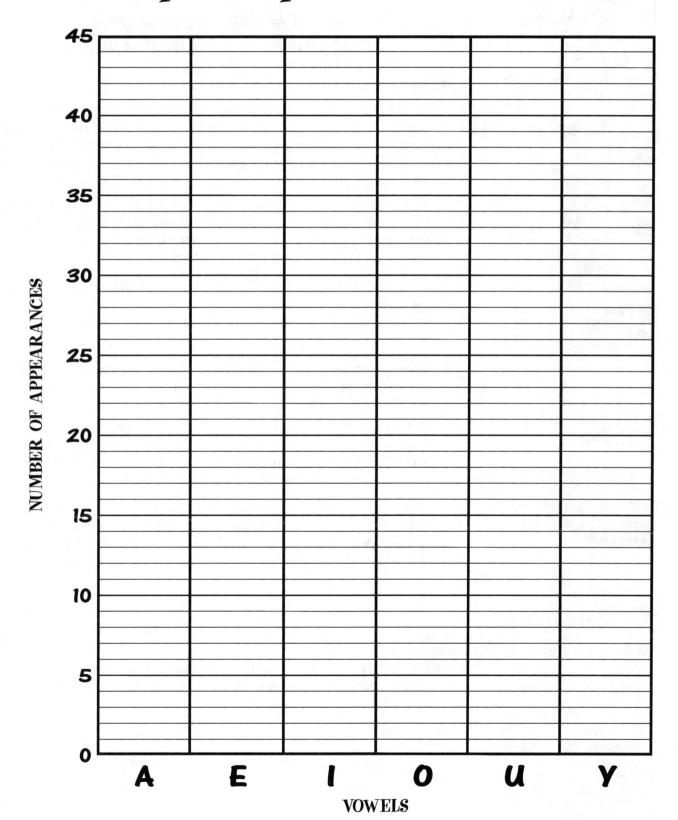

Sampling Cents

When you're studying a large group, taking a sample makes a lot of "cents"!

Grouping

Small groups

You'll Need

◆ Jar of pennies (or mixed coins)
◆ Paper
◆ Pencils

Teaching Tip

Make sure students are making a new tally mark each time they find a coin with the same year.

Writing Connection

Ask students to explain why sampling works. What can sampling tell about the larger group? What might be some drawbacks of sampling?

DIRECTIONS

1. Discuss the concept of sampling with students. Explain that TV ratings are created by taking a sample of the shows that a limited number of households are watching. Ask students why they think rating companies do this rather than ask every single person what shows he or she watches. After students have had a chance to respond, explain that taking a sample is a way to get information about a large group of people without having to study each one. By looking at a sample—a smaller part of the large group—we can get a good idea about the rest of the group.

2. Hold up the jar of coins. Tell students you want to find out when the coins were minted. A year is stamped on each coin. How could students find the years without looking at each and every coin?

3. Have one student from each group make a recording sheet on a blank piece of paper. Down the left side of the page, they should write the years, from Before 1970, 1970, 1971, up to the current year. Have another student in each group randomly take 30 coins from the jar. This will be the group's sample of coins. Have students look at the year stamped on each coin and make a tally mark next to that year on their recording sheet.

4. When everyone has completed this task, discuss the results as a class. Which year had the most tally marks? Which had the fewest? Were the results from each group similar? What would students predict about the rest of the pennies in the jar based on the results of the sample?

➡➡➡ EXTENSION

Have students make bar graphs or pictographs based on their sampling results. You may want to have students combine their results and graph the class data.

Clothing Combos

Students learn about combinations as they hang their clothes on a tree diagram.

PREPARATION

On the chalkboard, write three column headings: *Hats, Shirts,* and *Shoes.* Under *Hats,* write *Baseball Cap* and *Straw Hat.* Under *Shirts,* write *Red, Blue,* and *Green.* Under *Shoes,* write *Sneakers* and *Sandals.*

DIRECTIONS

1. Ask students to look at the list you've written on the chalkboard and tell you how many different outfits could be put together if each outfit was one hat, one shirt, and one pair of shoes. Give students a few minutes to work on the problem and let them make some guesses. If anyone comes up with the answer (12), ask the student to explain how he or she figured it out.

2. Tell students that one way to figure out the possible combinations is by making a tree diagram. Draw a tree diagram on the chalkboard to show the possible combinations of clothing. Explain that this tree diagram shows the 6 different combinations for one type of hat. The same combinations could be made for the other hat. Erase *Baseball Cap* from the tree diagram and write *Straw Hat* in its place. Show that there are 6 more combinations for the Straw Hat. Added together, there are 12 combinations.

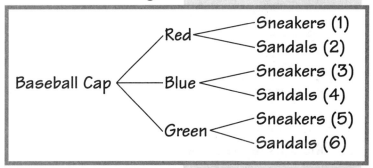

3. Have each student invent a character—a clown, sports figure, actress, etc. They should plan a wardrobe for this character consisting of 2 hats and 3 shirts. Ask students to draw a tree diagram to show the different possible clothing combinations. When students have mastered this simple tree diagram, they can expand the wardrobe with more items (hats, shirts, shoes, pants) and more choices per item.

 ASSESSMENT

Tell students there is a way to check the number of combinations they find: multiply together all the numbers of choices. For example, for 3 hats and 3 shirts there are 9 combinations.

 **Grouping**
Individual

You'll Need

◆ Clothing items—a few pairs of shoes, hats, shirts, etc. (Optional)

Name _____

Problems and More

Put on your thinking cap to solve these problems.

1. WORD PROBLEMS

The letters in these equations stand for real math words.

Example: 7 D = 1 W
Answer: 7 Days = 1 Week

How many can you solve?

12 I = 1 F _____

12 M = 1 Y _____

60 M = 1 H _____

16 O = 1 P _____

5 P = 1 N _____

36 I = 1 Y _____

2. "TRI" THIS

Move only three of the dots to make the triangle point in the opposite direction.

3. GIVE ME A SIGN

Fill the ○ with + and − signs to make this equation true:

4 ○ 3 ○ 7 ○ 5 ○ 8 ○ 2 = 9

Now make your own mystery equation.

4. CUBE QUIZ

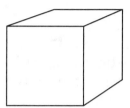

Look at this cube. Write the total number of

a. faces _____

b. edges _____

c. corners _____

(Hint: Don't forget the parts you can't see!)

5. GETTING A-ROUND TO THE POINT

How many lines will it take to connect every point on the circle to every other point on it? Do you see a pattern? What if the circle had 6 points?

_____

6. A HEAVY QUESTION

Which weighs more: a pound of feathers or a pound of iron?

_____

An Assessment Toolkit

Alternative methods of assessment provide a comprehensive profile for each student. As students work on *50+ Super-Fun Math Activities: Grade 4*, here are some ways you might observe and record their work. Alone or in combination, they can provide a quick snapshot that will add to your knowledge of students' development in mathematics. They also give you concrete observations to share with families at reporting time.

FILE CARDS

An alphabetical file system, with a card for each student, provides a handy way to keep notes on students' progress. Choose a few students each day that you plan to observe. Pull their cards, jot down the date and activity, and record comments about their work.

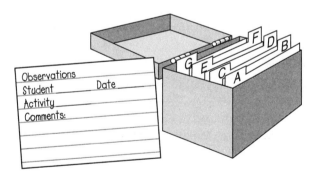

CLIPBOARDS

With a list of students attached to your clipboard, you can easily move about the classroom and jot down observations about their work and their thinking. If you want to focus on a particular skill or competency, you can create a quick checklist and simply check as you observe.

STICKY NOTES

As you circulate while individuals or small groups are working, create a sticky note for students who show particular strengths or areas for your attention and help. Be sure to date the note. The advantage to this technique is that you can move the notes to a record folder to create a profile; you can also cluster students with similar competencies as a reminder for later grouping.

CHECKLISTS AND RUBRICS

On Pages 62 and 63, you'll find a few ready-made checklists and a rubric. Feel free to modify them to suit your own needs. Invite students to assess their own work—they are honest and insightful, and you'll have another perspective on their mathematical development!

Name _____ Date _____

Self-Evaluation Form

ACTIVITY _____

1. The activity was **(HARD EASY)** to complete because _____

_____

_____

2. The part of the activity I did best was _____

_____

_____

3. I could have done a better job if _____

_____

_____

4. The mathematics I used was _____

_____

_____

5. After completing the activity I felt _____

   because _____

_____

_____

6. I would rate my work on the activity as **(EXCELLENT GOOD FAIR POOR)**

   because _____

_____

_____

50+ Super-Fun Math Activities: Grade 4 © 2010 by Scholastic Inc.

Assessment Checklist

Activity _____ Date _____ Group _____

Students					
MATHEMATICS KNOWLEDGE					
Understands problem or task					
Formulates and carries out a plan					
Explains concepts clearly					
Uses models or tools appropriately					
Makes connections to similar problems					
Can create similar problems					
MATHEMATICAL PROCESSES					
Justifies responses logically					
Listens carefully to others and evaluates information					
Reflects on and explains procedures					
LEARNING DISPOSITIONS					
Tackles difficult tasks					
Perseveres					
Shows confidence in own ability					
Collaborates/shares ideas					

SCORING RUBRIC

3 Fully accomplishes the task

Shows full understanding of the central mathematical idea(s)

Communicates thinking clearly using oral explanation or written, symbolic, or visual means

2 Partially accomplishes the task

Shows partial understanding of the central mathematical idea(s)

Written or oral explanation partially communicates thinking, but may be incomplete, misdirected, or not clearly presented

1 Does not accomplish the task

Shows little or no grasp of the central mathematical idea(s)

Recorded work or oral explanation is fragmented and not understandable

Answers to Problems and More

PAGES 32-33

1. Here is one way to complete the square. (Students may invert the rows and columns.)

6	1	8
7	5	3
2	9	4

2. 8 dimes, 4 nickels, and 7 pennies

3. Here is one way to "connect the dots":

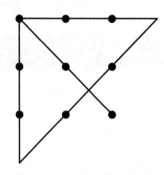

4. ShOES (53045)

5. E, N, T (one, two, three, four, five, six, seven, eight, nine, ten)

6. Here is one way to solve the puzzle: Move the dime to B, penny to C, dime to C, nickel to B, dime to A, penny to B, dime to B, quarter to C, dime to C, penny to A, dime to A, nickel to C, dime to B, penny to C, and dime to C.

7. Take away the "s"!

8. 13 triangles.

9. $2 = 5 - 3$

PAGE 60

1. 12 Inches = 1 Foot; 12 Months = 1 Year; 60 Minutes = 1 Hour; 16 Ounces = 1 Pound (or 1 Pint); 5 Pennies = 1 Nickel; 36 Inches = 1 Yard

2.

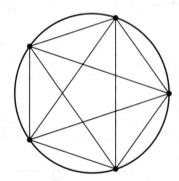

3. $4 - 3 + 7 - 5 + 8 - 2 = 9$

4. 6 faces, 12 edges, 8 corners

5. 10 lines

6. They both weigh the same—one pound!